GW00362976

Purple Ronnie's
Star Signs

Leo

23rd July - 22nd August

☆

First published 1994 by Statics(London) Ltd

This edition published 2002 by Boxtree
an imprint of Pan Macmillan Ltd
Pan Macmillan, 20 New Wharf Road, London N1 9RR
Basingstoke and Oxford
Associated companies throughout the world
www.panmacmillan.com

ISBN 0 7522 2036 5

9 8 7 6 5 4 3 2 1

A CIP catalogue record for this book is available from
the British Library

Text by Giles Andreae
Illustrations by Janet Cronin
Printed and bound in Hong Kong

☆ Introduction ☆

Star Signs are a brilliant way of finding out about someone's character. You can use them to discover anything you like including what everyone's secretest rude fantasies are.

But reading what's written in the stars can only be done by incredibly brainy people like me. After gazing for ages through my gigantic telescope and doing loads of complicated sums and

charts and stuff I have been able to
work out exactly what everyone in the
world is really like.

This book lets you know about all my
amazing discoveries. It tells you what you
look like, who your friends are, how your
love life is, what you're like at Doing It
and who you should be Doing It with.

Everything I've written in this book is
completely true. Honest.

Love from

Purple Ronnie
xox

Contents

They like to have fun
and be happy
They're carefree and
noisy and proud
They sing naughty
songs at the top
of their voices
And never stop farting
out loud

- botty burner special

Leo Looks

Leos love it when
people look at them so
they always try to be as
gorgeous and beautiful
as they can

Leo Men

Leo Men are often tall and thin with strong muscles. They have loud voices and giant doodahs

Leo Women

Leo Women have beautiful faces, sexy eyes and loads of long wavy hair. They like to dress up in saucy undies

Leo Character

Leos are the happiest and smiliest people in the world. What they like most is partying, being silly and having fun

yeh!

But sometimes, especially when they have drunk loads of booze, Leos can turn into loud bossy show-offs

Leo and Friends

Leos have loads of mates

for mucking around with...

... but only one or two
bestest friends
for sharing their
special secrets with

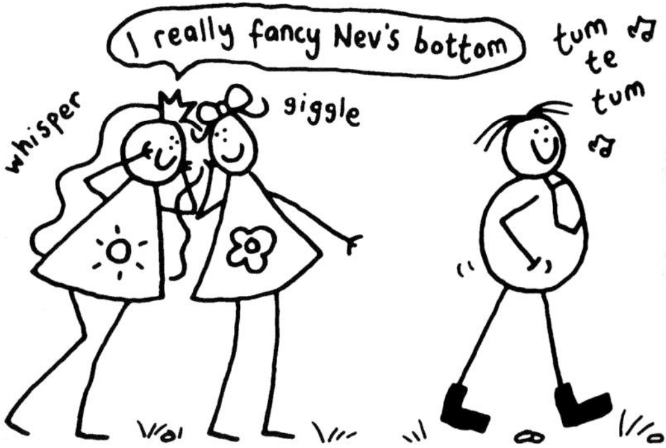
I really fancy Nev's bottom
whisper
giggle
tum te tum

POP STARS

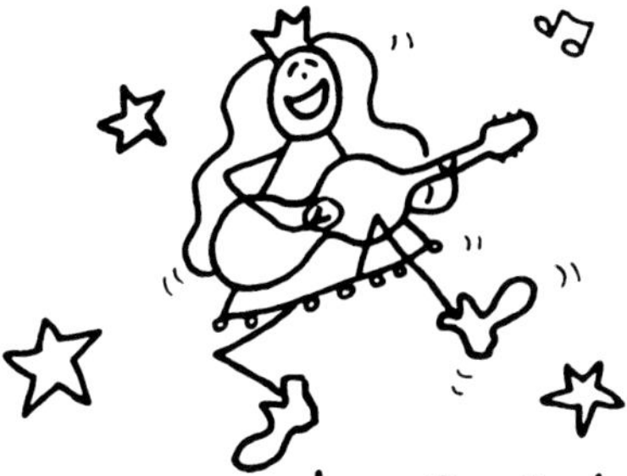

because:-

1. They like people to tell them how fantastic they are

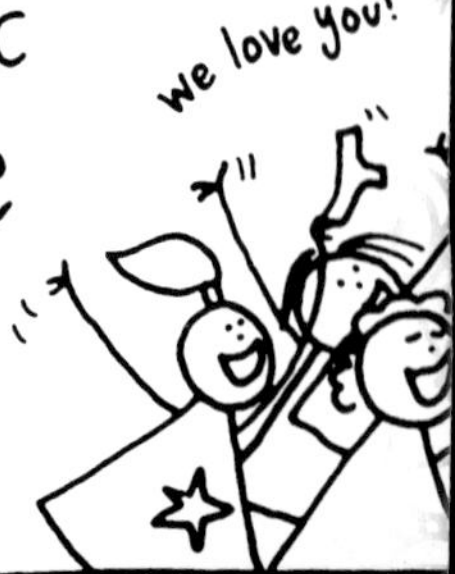

3. They love
leaping around
and making
lots of noise

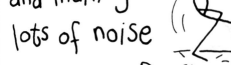

stamp

Leo and Love

Leo is the most romantic star sign of all and people who are Leos fall <u>very deeply</u> in love

A Leo who loves you will give you millions of presents and won't ever think of Doing It with anyone else EVER

Warning:-

If you do not love a Leo as much as a Leo loves you his heart will be broken for ever

Leo and Sex

Leos love:-

STROKING

TIC

HUGGING

When it comes to
Doing It Leos always
like to be in charge

☆ Special Tip ☆

A Leo who wants
you for sex will want
you for love and
friendship as well

The End